Animals

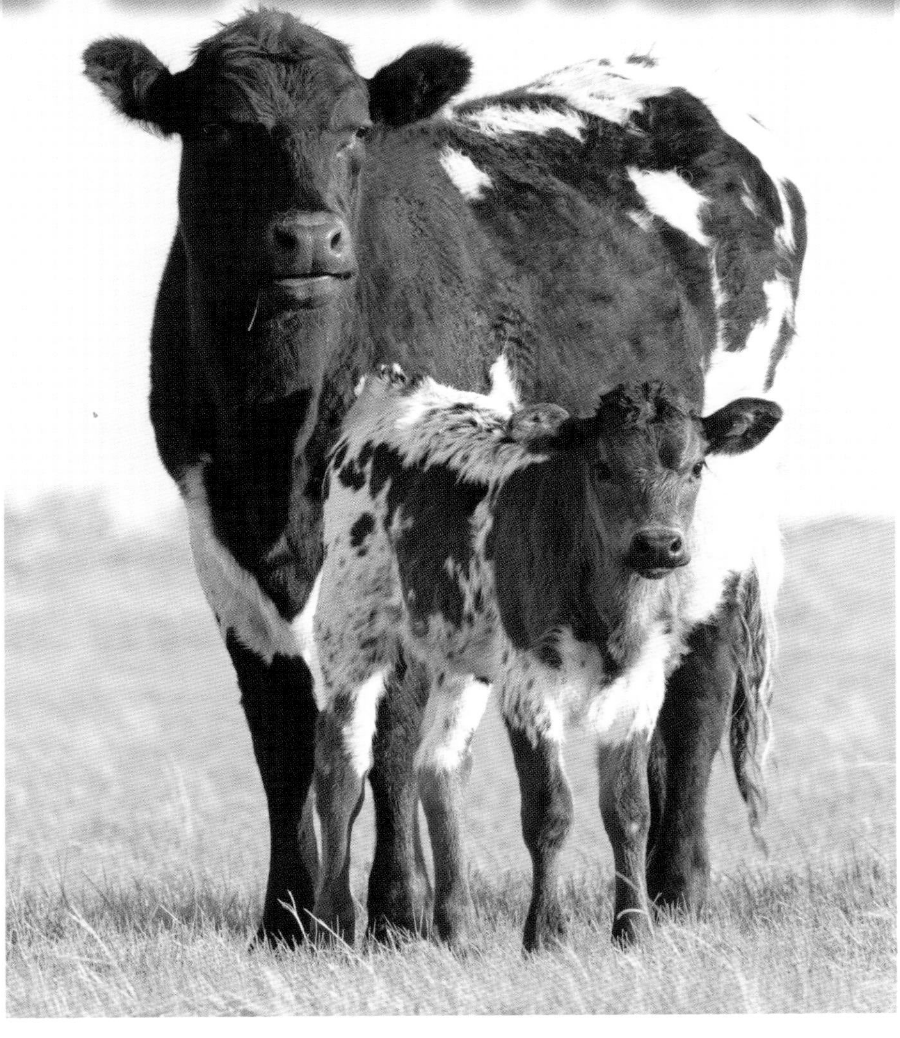

Stephanie Reid

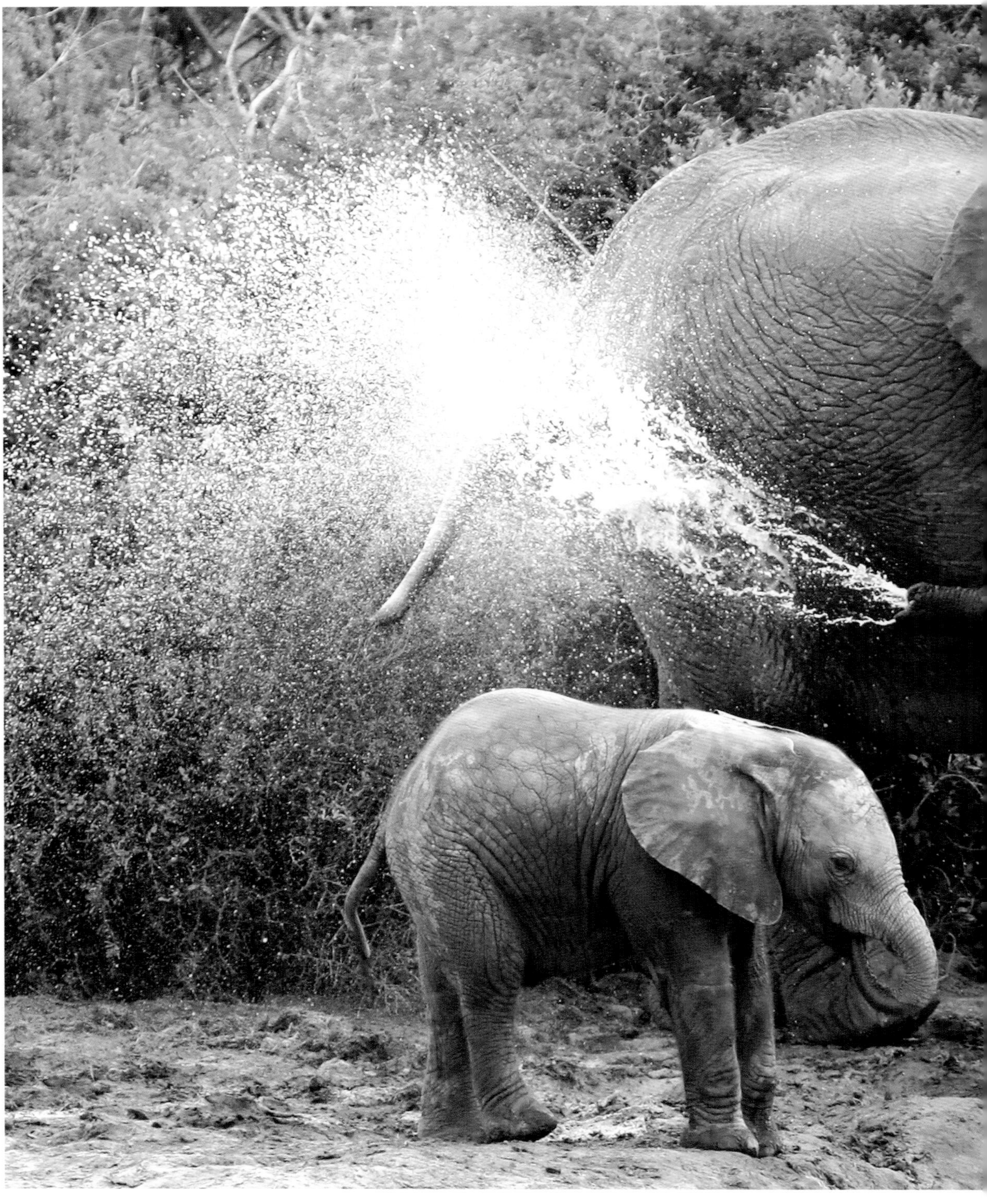

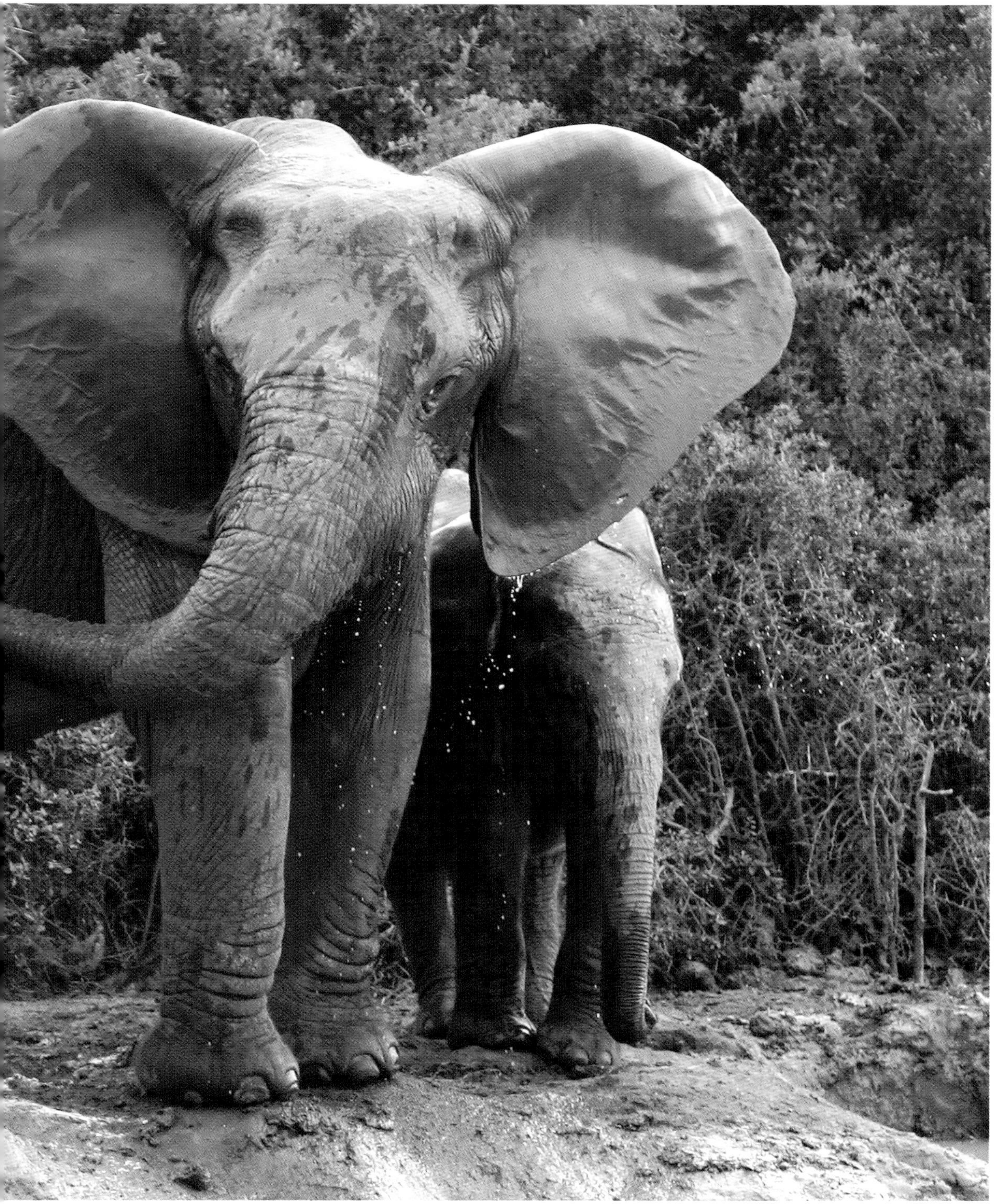

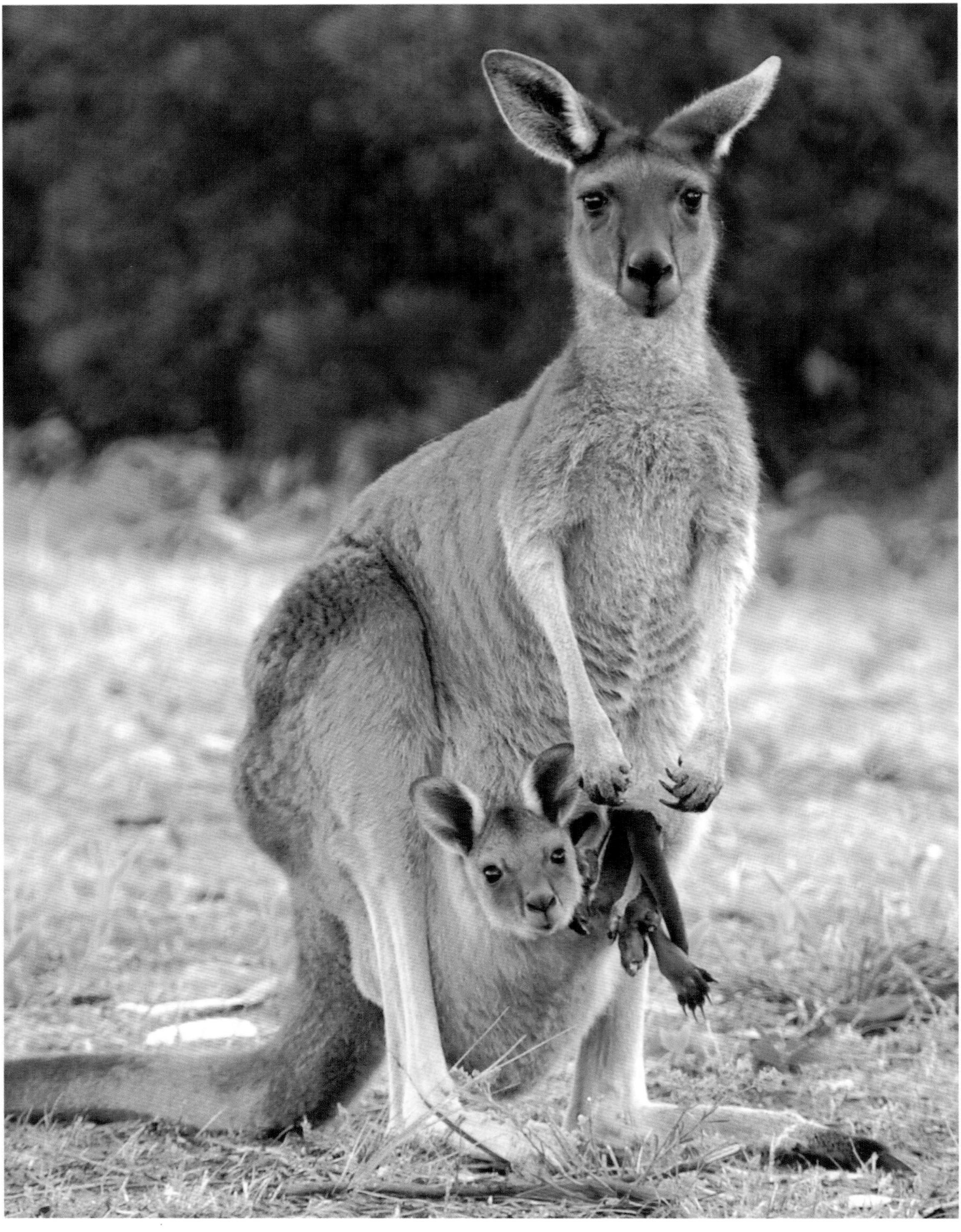

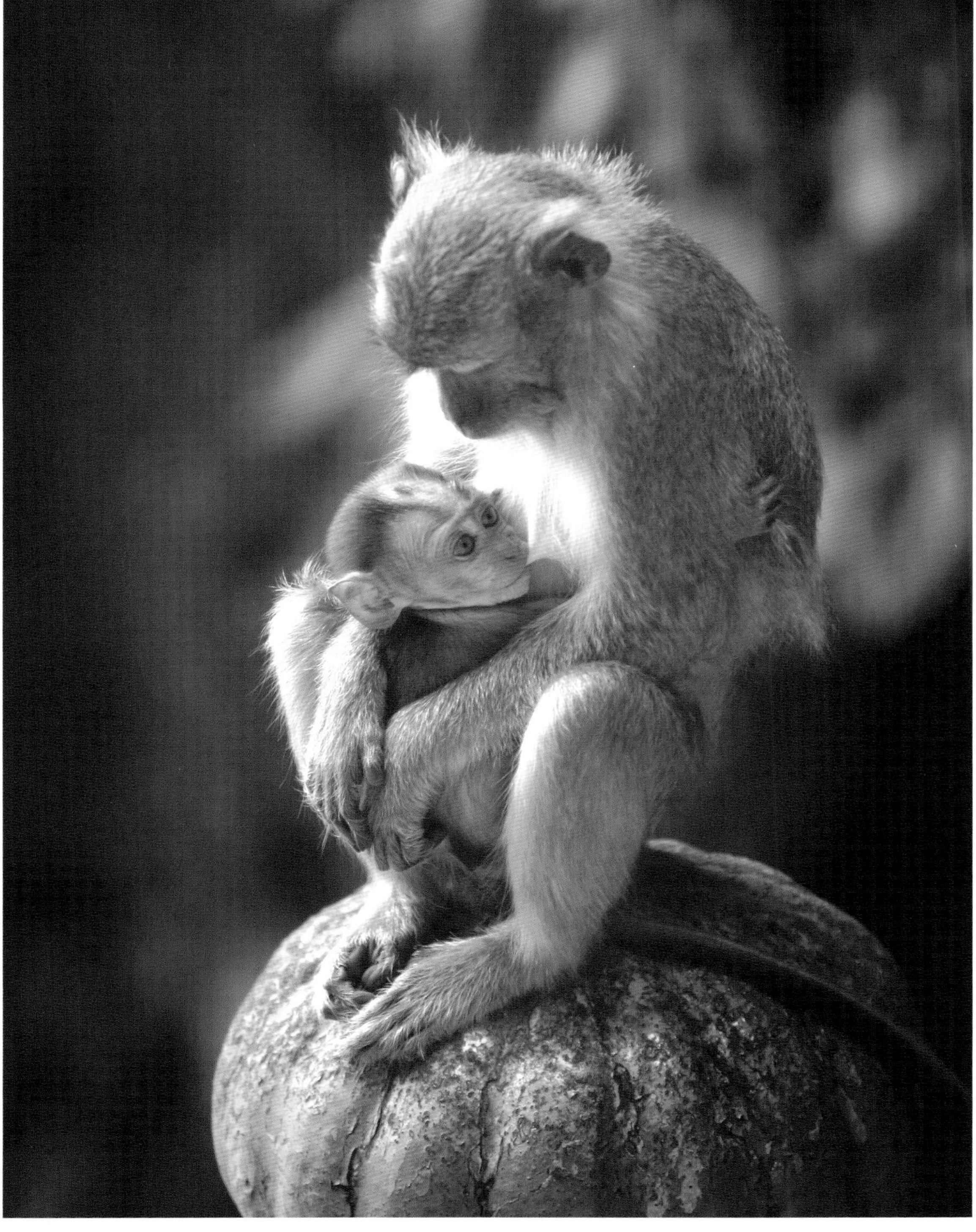

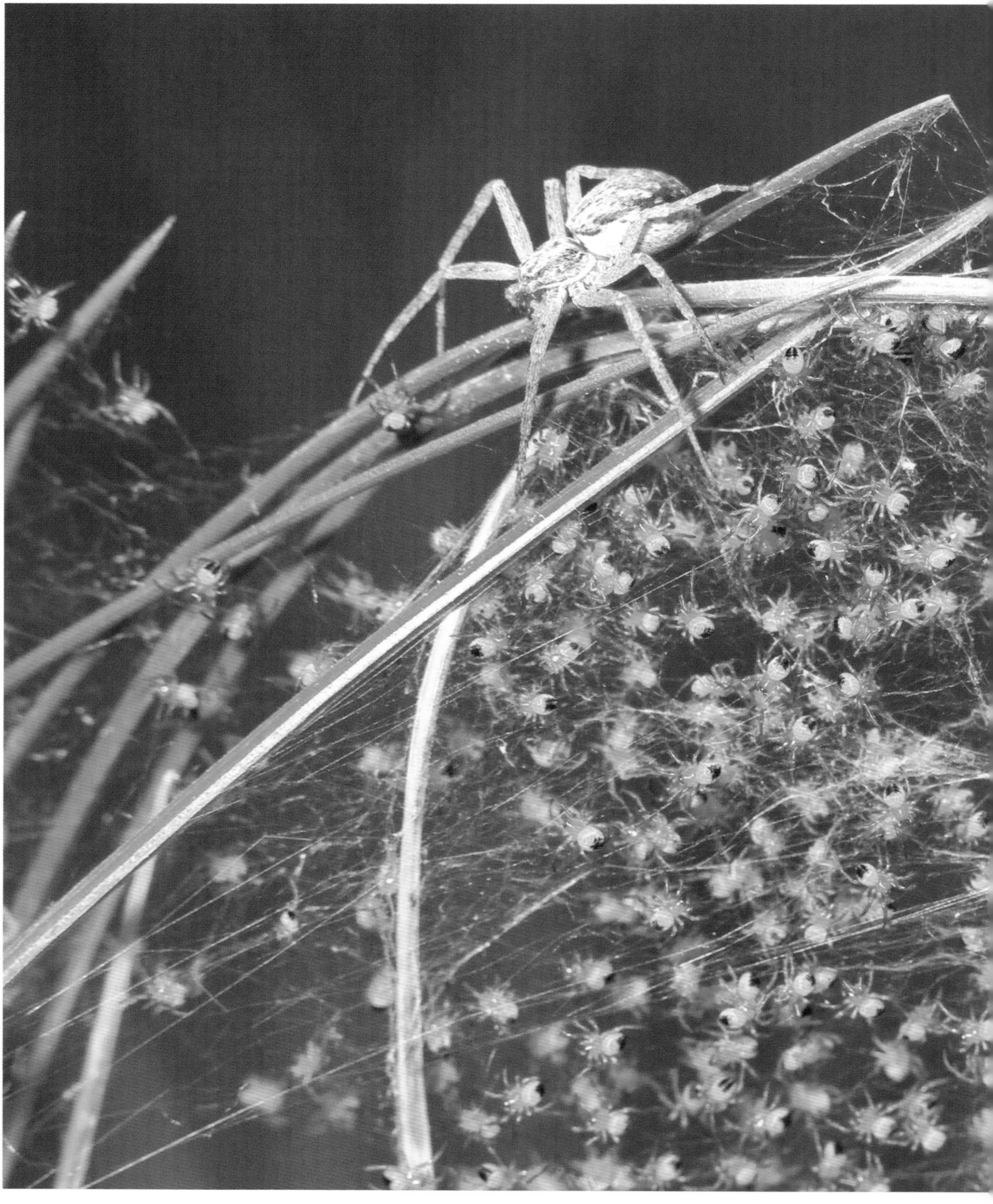

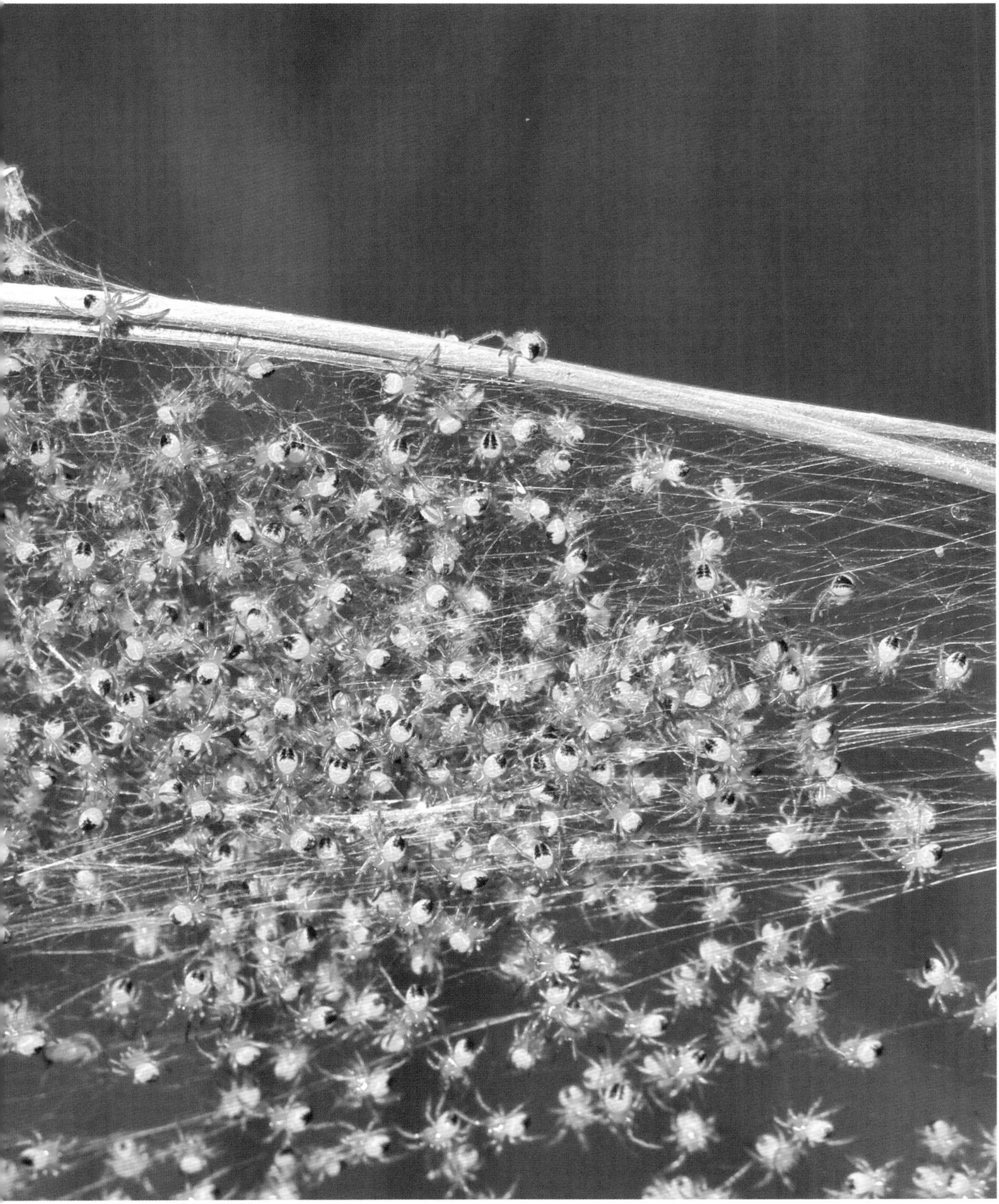

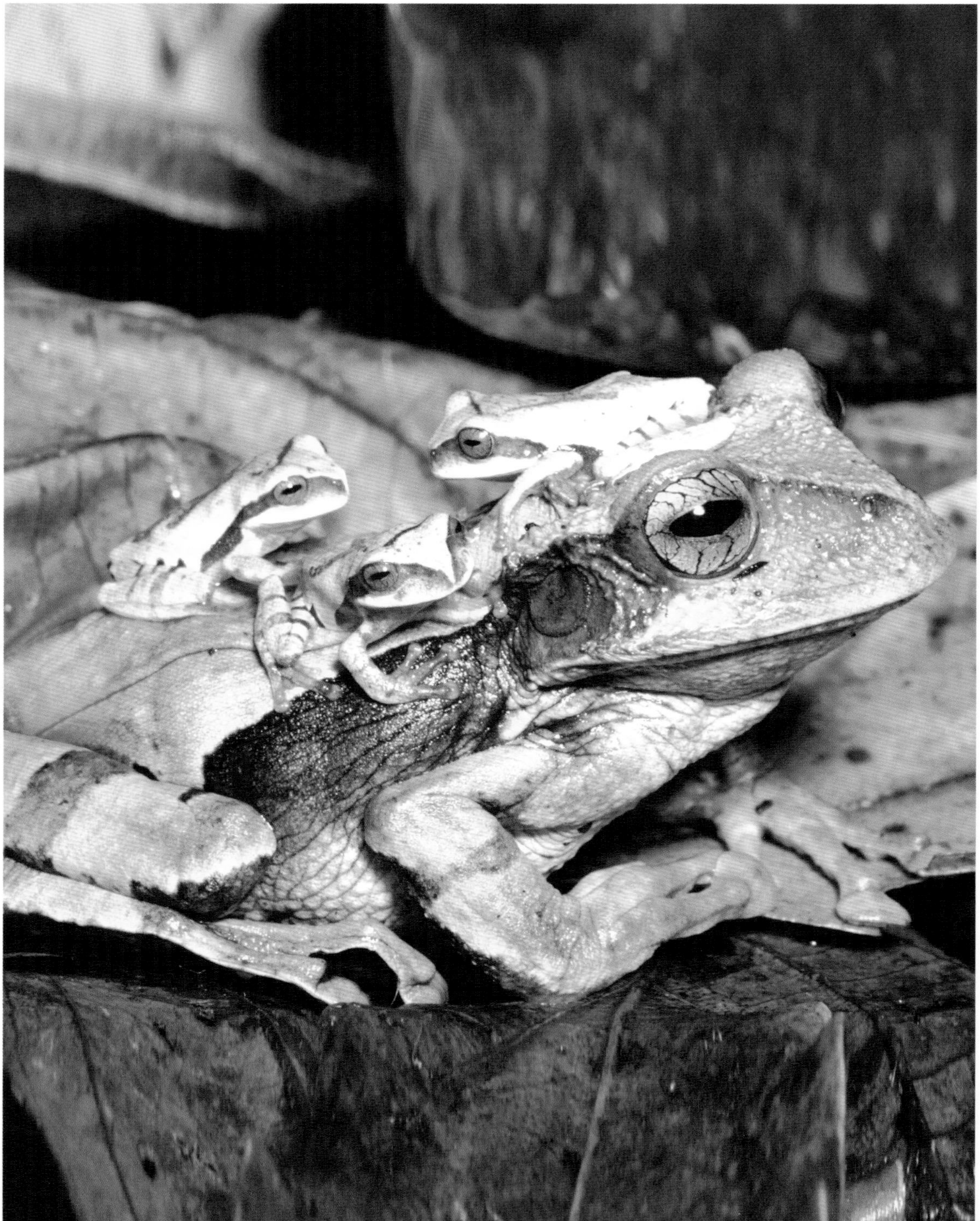

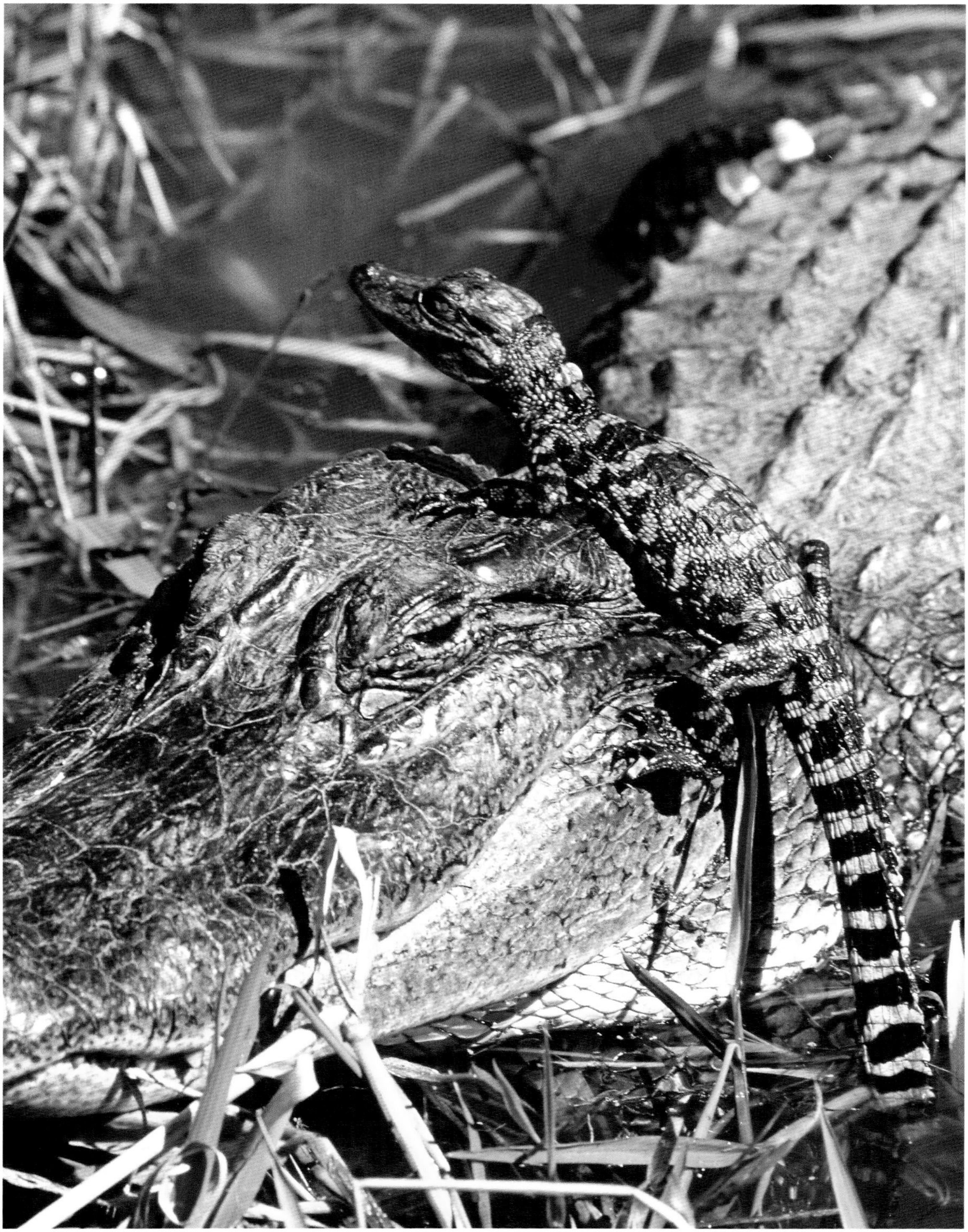

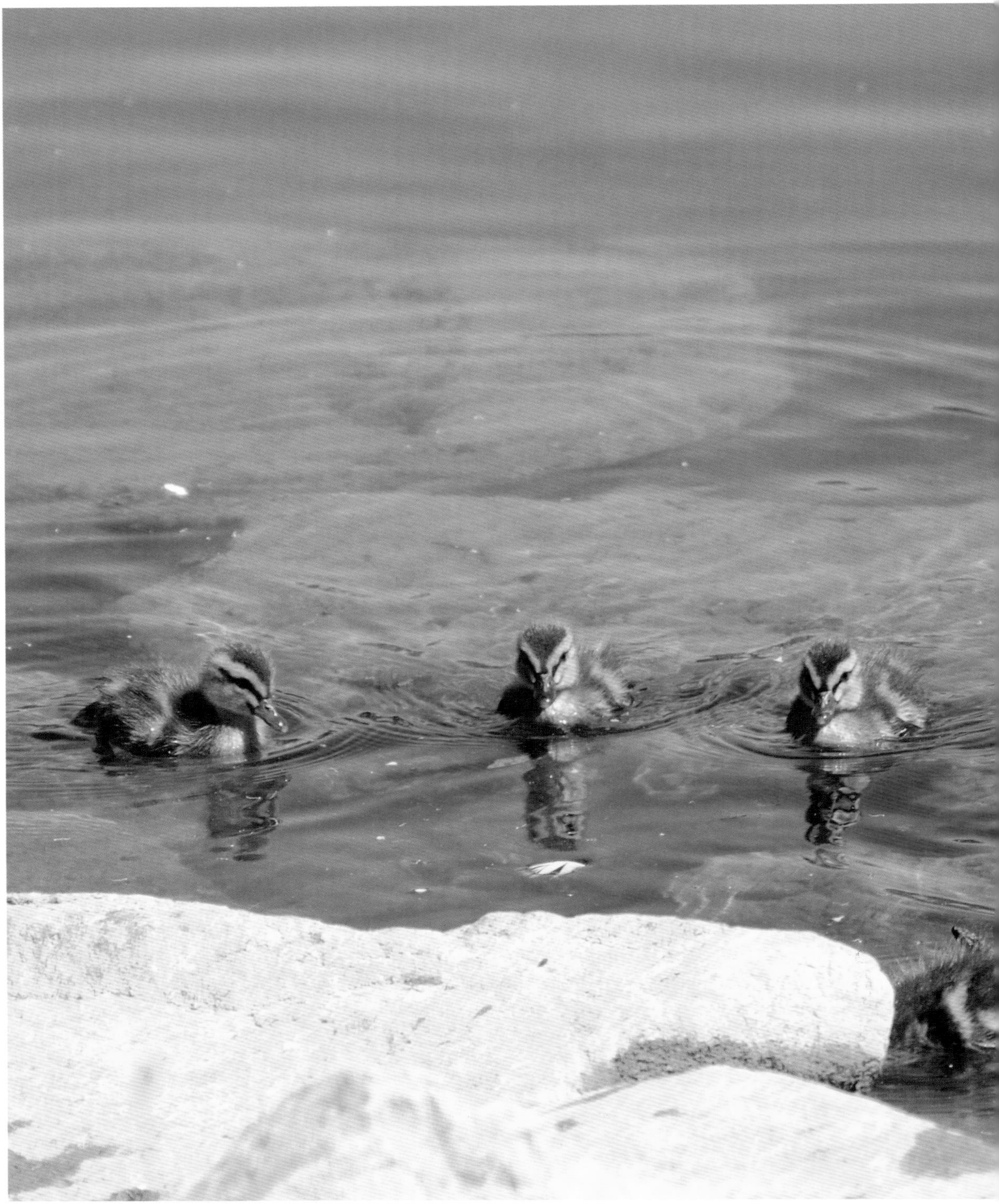

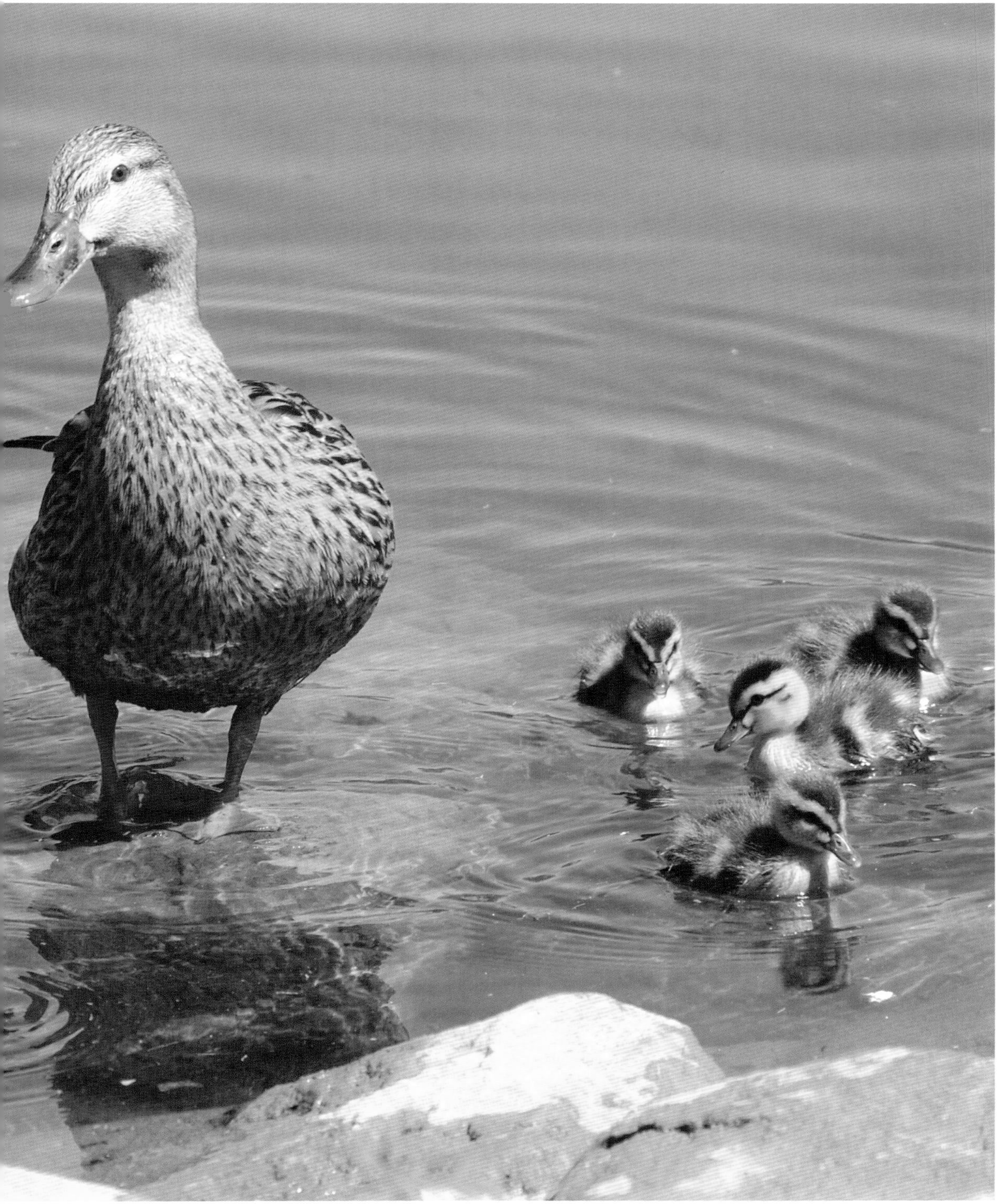

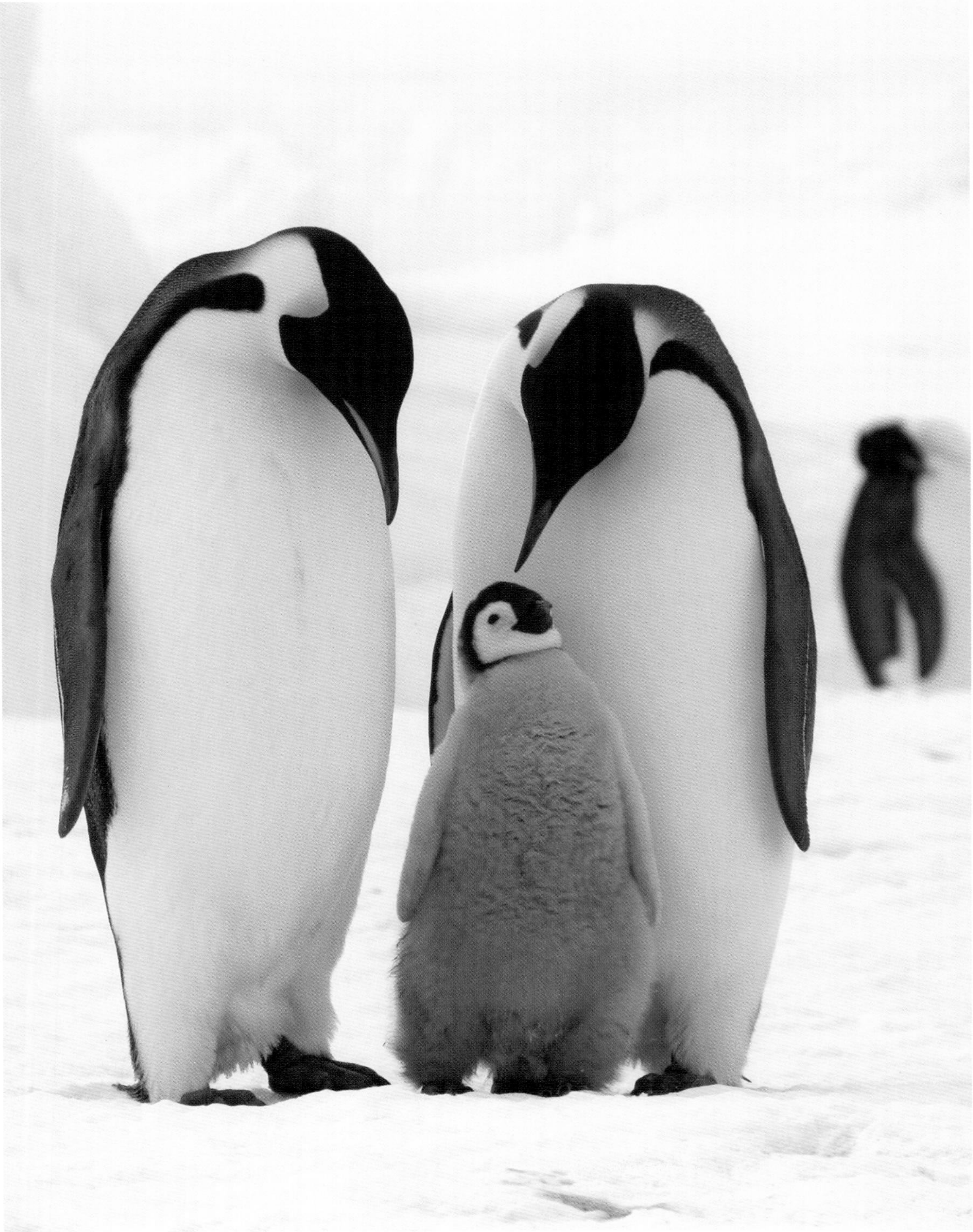

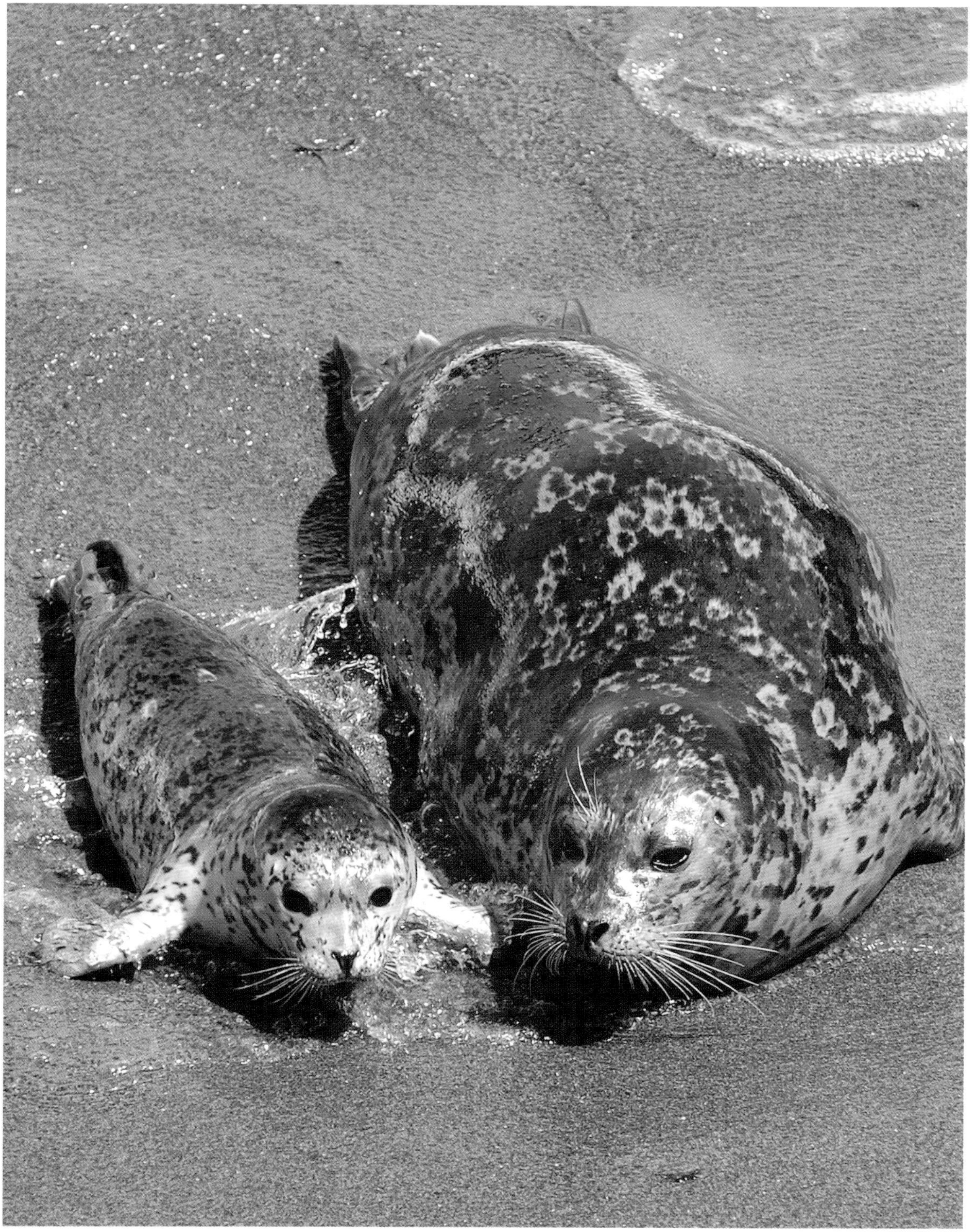

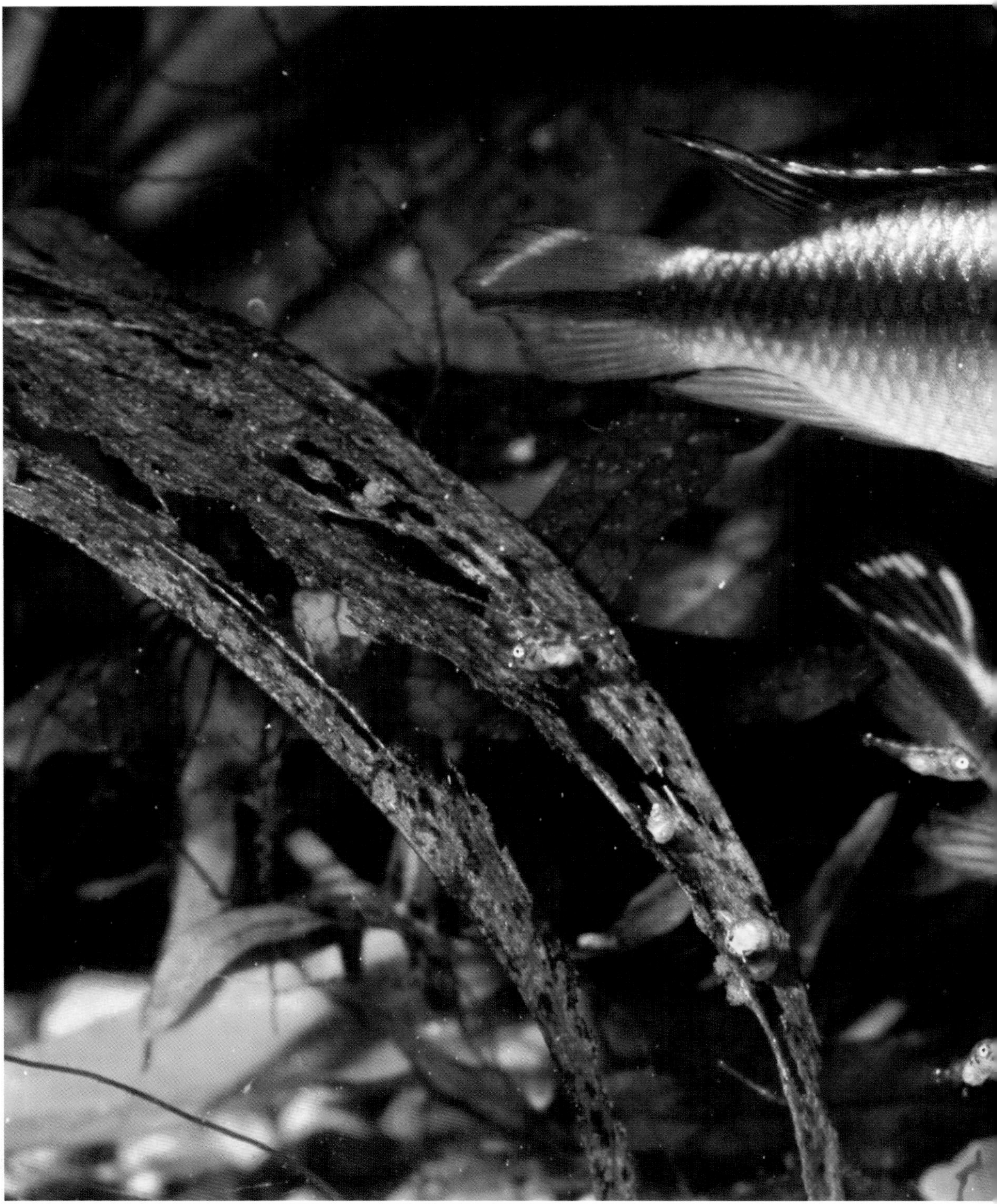

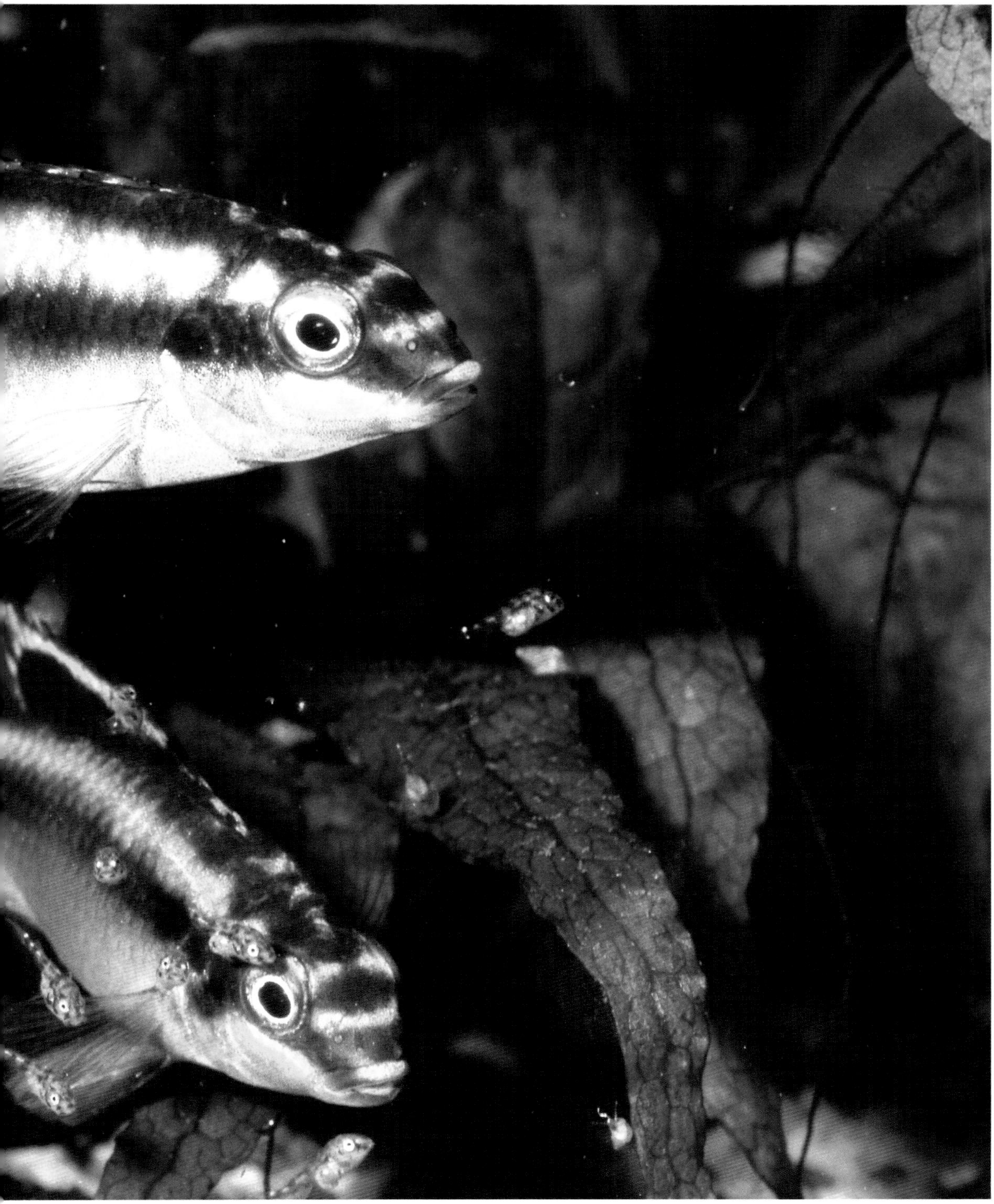

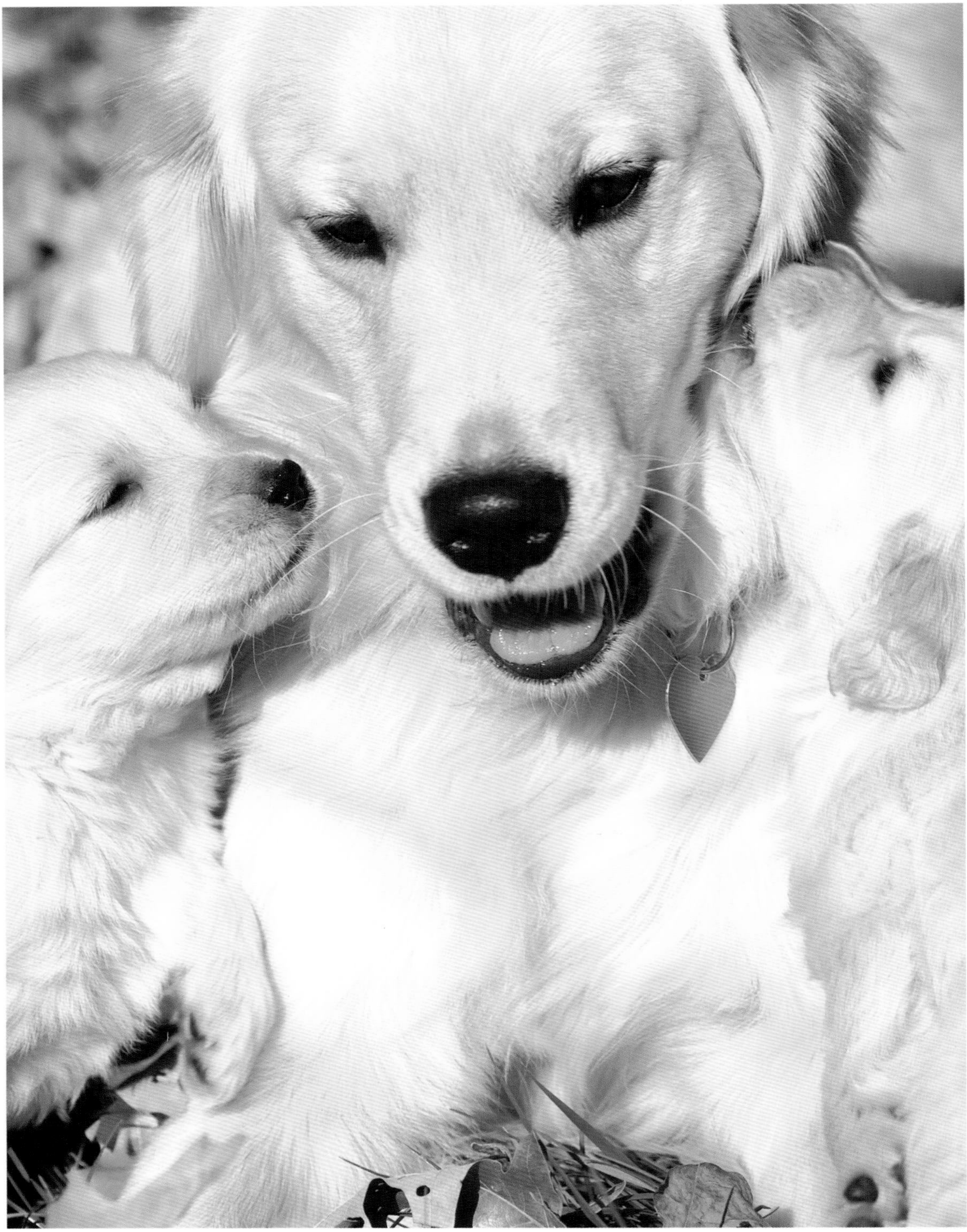